# POPULAR PARENTING METHODS

## Are They Really Working?

### Time for CPR:
# A CULTURAL PARENTING REVOLUTION

NICHOLEEN PECK

# DEDICATION

For parents everywhere who have
tried giving in, who have tried getting upset,
and who are still thinking there must be
a better way to parent children.
This book will help you deliberately
choose what parenting model is best for you and
your family, and stop all the guess work.

# CONTENTS

# ACKNOWLEDGMENTS

Because a man named Mark Wanstall wrote an article called
*What Can We Learn From the World's Strictest Parents,* I found a
phrase I had been looking for for years. Thank you Mark. I don't
know you. You don't know me. But, your thoughts have given me
a few vocabulary words I was searching for.

Beverly Arbon, SherLynne Beach and Sherry Bowthorpe all
helped in creating this book. I am so grateful for dear friends
who make projects like this possible.

Mostly I would like to thank my family, who is my
self-government teaching team. They live the things I teach and
now even teach them with me. We are free to love, laugh and live
as a united family because my family has been freed from emotional bondage
by learning self-government principles.
I never thought life and parenting could be so happy!

# INTRODUCTION

When my two oldest children were babies I was overwhelmed. Tantrums, messes, whining and hitting happened all day every day. I used any "trick" I could gather from magazines or friendly conversations, but nothing really helped me have the kind of home I wanted. I wanted a certain kind of feeling. I knew it was possible. I had read old stories about families and they left me feeling connected and contented. That was what I wanted for my family too.

Then I decided to do foster care for troubled teens so that I could stay home with my two young babies while my husband went back to school. Foster care is not for the lazy parent. I knew that. It was an experience which changed my life forever. In fact, often times with two babies and two teenagers out of control, I felt like I was drowning. When I brought those wonderfully complicated and broken feeling souls into my home I learned to love in a different way and communicate in a different way. In order to help them embrace happiness I had to teach them self-government. They needed structure and principles which would protect them in all their future relationships.

Anne Sullivan said, "Obedience is the gateway through which knowledge enters the mind of a child." I have found this to be true especially when speaking of the knowledge of love and the knowledge of happiness. Security and happiness are made in structured, loving environments where parents strictly follow principles. In fact, happiness enters more than the mind of a child, it enters the child's heart. Which, after all, is the place where change occurs. When we reach the hearts of our children they choose the freedom which comes only through self-government.

This is the reason for this book –to help us examine our parenting choices and look closely where those choices will lead our children. Are they self-governing now? Will they be trained to be self-governing as adults? If not, it is time for a Cultural Parenting Revolution in your home. This book will give you insight into examining what may need to change.

# PART 1

# QUESTIONING POPULAR PARENTING

# 1

# WHAT ARE THE
# THREE CORE PARENTING STYLES?

### Living My Regular Life on TV

A few years ago we had the opportunity to welcome a couple of very troubled British teenagers into our home as a television experiment because our family was "traditional", religious, and quite strict. The BBC came over from England and documented our family dynamics on video because these types of TV shows are widely popular in England. I also believe they were hoping to see some yelling, some demands, some major confrontations, and total disharmony and collapse of the family structure.

But when the show, which was called *The World's Strictest Parents*, aired in the UK, it surprisingly became "the most watched episode ever on the BBC." according to the program producers. The viewers witnessed no yelling, no demands, no major confrontations (or minor ones), and, to their surprise, our family stayed intact and calm. This really puzzled the viewers and the critics.

Mark Wanstall, a British reporter/critic, wrote an article called "What Can We Learn From *The World's Strictest Parents?*" One of the first things he said was that parents are going about parenting all wrong, that the traditionally strict model, which *was* the style in our family dynamics, has been lost to "modern progressive parenting." This made me think about some of the episodes on this show that I had watched earlier. Some parents were very confrontational, aggressive, and angry. Their attitude was power – the one with the most power won the battle -- while other parents were so laid back that they allowed the children to do whatever they wanted. They had the attitude that the child should decide everything without any, or very little, direction from the parents. This later style of parenting is the modern progressive philosophy of parenting.

It seems that parenting methods go in cycles. Strauss and Howe, authors of the book *The Fourth Turning*, identified four main types of people who have specific characteristics which identify with others of their generational type from generations before them. One of these generational types of people who show up every 80 years or so is the "Hero Generation." This is the generation of people who fought in WWII and the Revolutionary war. If Strauss and Howe are correct, then we are raising "Hero Generation" children and youth right now. We should learn from the parents of the last "Hero Generation."

In the early 1900's the "Hero Generation" were the children of traditional strict parents. After WWII, the parenting culture changed partially because the American families were more in survival mode. There were fewer fathers, so mothers had to work, and much of the day-to-day family responsibilities landed on the children. Gradually, to maintain control, parenting became more aggressive; discipline became harsh. I call this type of parenting bullying, fear-based parenting. Notice, the busier the families were, the more desperate the discipline measures felt.

Dr. Spock, a very popular post WWII parenting guru, swung the parenting pendulum into the extreme opposite of aggression, one of telling children nothing and allowing them to find their own direction. His philosophy was that the parents should not be parents, but their children's friends instead. His books became the standard, were quoted widely, and parenting changed drastically. This was the "birth" of the hippie generation full of "enlightened" individuals who did "their own thing" in every aspect of life.

This type of parenting is about as dangerous as the over-powerful, aggressive kind. Mr. Wanstall suggested that societies should re-establish the traditional strict type of parenting. However, the word "strict" often implies the aggressive, damaging type of discipline, but that is not what traditional strict parenting is. In Webster's 1828 dictionary, the word "strict" means "governed by a certain set of principles." So strict is good! Traditional strict parenting values the individual and at the same time has rules to be taught and followed. A wise friend of mine said that "a strict parent doesn't have to be mean or yell." How true!

## 2

## TWO ESSENTIAL KEYS TO
## PARENTING SUCCESS

As we look at these three methodologies: Traditional Strict, Modern Progressive, and Bullying Fear-based (aggressive) – it is important to remember two key principles:

1.        Parents must *deliberately* and *consciously* make choices for their families. If they don't, that void will most likely be filled with popular agendas formulated by smart, clever, and misdirected experts.

2.        Parents are the ones to decide what is best for their families' physical, emotional, and spiritual welfare – no one else -- not the government, not school teachers or church leaders. Parents should look within themselves for the answers for their families because the dynamics and the personalities are different in each home. Therefore, they need to be aware of what is happening in the home in order to decide what needs to be changed.

These two points provide a starting place for parents who are looking for stability and direction for their families. The parents who are invited to participate on The BBC's *World's Strictest Parents* program recognize these principles as essential parenting paradigms for family success. And, furthermore, the communities of families they belong to usually support strict parenting because they also see the power and confidence parents must have to guide their children to happy productive lifestyles. Even if the parents on the show were aggressive, bully-type parents, they still understood these two vital principles. You, as the parent, get to choose, and you, the parent, knows what's best for your family. Once you have made a conscious, deliberate choice to lead your family, you need to have a plan for family unity and close relationships.

Our family's plan is to learn self-government and practice it together while working on strengthening family relationships as described in the book *Parenting A House United*. "Self-government is being able to determine the cause and effect in any given situation, and possessing a knowledge of your own behaviors so that you can control them." *(Parenting A House United)*

## A Need For Change

In his article, Mr. Wanstall, stated that there is an "emptying out of the adult identity" going on in the world today. Adults feel powerless. They generally don't feel very confident about parenting. They don't know how to do it, so they want someone else or some agency to do it for them, even sending their children to *The World's Strictest Parents* show if necessary.

With child-rearing methods flip-flopping so much, adults are afraid to say or do anything when they see delinquent behavior in children, both in their own or someone else's. Some adults do not understand what their real identity and responsibilities are, and they are afraid their standards might be wrong in our ever-shifting societies.

The first change we, as parents, should make is to consciously choose to be proactive. Decide what principles and standards *your* family will live by and take action. Furthermore, if you love people and care about your society and its future, choose to make a difference when you see something obviously wrong in someone's behavior; even if they don't live with you. Correction can be done calmly and with love in the way a good parent would do. Here is an example:

We had hired a young 21-year-old man to do some sheet-rock work for us. When he was done, he said that he was going to bid on a job at our neighbor's place. Before he left, I told him, " I want to give you a little piece of advice. If we hadn't already known you, we would not have hired you for this job because of your disrespectful appearance. Your pants are too low. So before you go over there, you probably should pull up your pants. You'll have a better chance of getting the job." He had not thought of that, pulled them up, tightened his belt, and got the job. That is kind assertiveness.

How does this apply to our own families? How we were raised determines how we will raise our children. For example, I was raised in a bullying and fear-based, or aggressive, household. When my father declared that he was "the boss" (and he meant it!), I asked him why. His standard answer was, "Because I'm the dad, I'm the boss, and that's the way it's going to be." Why was he that way? Simple. His parents did not want to go along with the Dr. Spock theories of non-parenting, so they raised him in the opposite way because they knew no other.

It is natural for people to see one way of interacting as extreme and to assume that going to the extreme other direction is the solution to the parenting problem. However this is not going to solve the problem anymore than the other side of the manipulation measuring stick. The question should not be what way do we manipulate the children so that they do what we say? The question should be what principles do we focus on to touch the children's hearts so that they will be changed and improved forever.

There is no measuring stick for changing hearts. The process is so incremental and so personal it cannot be measured. It is inside the person. The parent and the child are both focusing on what is happening inside himself and the other person. It is an attachment action which creates lasting family connections. And, these connections happen when a child chooses obedience and is praised, and when a child chooses disobedience and needs correction. In both these situations the focus is the connection.

# PART 2

# THE THREE CORE PARENTING STYLES

## Which One Do You Now Use?

# 3

# HOW DO THE
# THREE PARENTING STYLES DIFFER?

To gain further understanding of what category of parent we fall into and where we can change for the better, it is necessary to discuss in more depth the differences between modern progressive (lenient), bullying fear-based (aggressive), and traditional strict (principled) parenting styles.

## Modern Progressive Parenting

Progressive means to move on; to abandon the past as if it does not exist. There are progressive businesses and progressive technologies. Progressive does have a positive meaning and often has good outcomes when used in many fields. However, it can be negative as well. In this parenting style, the children have total choice and very few guidelines, if any. Most parents who choose modern progressive parenting know they don't want their children to be afraid of them. They want happiness and they want the child to feel free. These are great goals.

| Parenting Forms | Mode & Movement | Leadership Structure | Teaching |
|---|---|---|---|
| **Modern Progressive** Destructive Form | Move-on progress Improve on the past Cultural revolution-destroy the past. Passive parenting, loss of parental power and role. | Child Led Parent manages-facilitates entertainment and opportunities Tyranny | No right or wrong Subjectivism Society is the authority figure to determine right and wrong Legalism-is it legal? Goal-independent |
| **Bullying Fear-based** Destructive Form | Move backward-regress Animalistic survival of the fittest Power-based aggressive | No Leader Parent enforces – using force, compulsion Us against Them Tyranny | Definite right and wrong determined by Parent Positive Legalism – is it legal according to this ruler? Goal: co-Dependent |
| **Traditional Strict** Constructive Form | Move in – to the heart, relationship-based Historical Moral order Moral guide Principle-based | Parent Led and Modeled | Right and wrong determined by principle – Core book Moralism – Higher authority Goal – interdependent |

| Foundation Principle and Effect | Focus | Agency | Parenting Action |
|---|---|---|---|
| Entitlement Free from correction Result – confusion, lonely, burdened Too many choices No guidelines Identity-based No identity | SELF Discovery | False Agency License Choice without consequences – disconnect Unpredictable Trial and error | Ignoring Pastoral – wild Uncultivated Unrestrained Unproductive Water – go with the flow |
| Punishment Anger – based Result – fear, dishonesty, distrust | SELF Preservation | No Agency Conformity No choice Unpredictable – trial and error | Requiring Hunter – gatherer Demanding benefit without planting and nurturing, consumptive Rock – unyielding |
| Consequence Cause and effect Result – free, safe, love, connection, order | FAMILY Unity | True Agency – Liberty Choice with knowledge of consequences Predictability | Training Inspiring Georgic – planning, planting, nurturing, productive, cultivated Soil, nourishing |

The only problem is that freedom doesn't come from leniency. Freedom is born from self-awareness, self-restraint, self-motivation, and self-government. The kind of self-government which can make a person, or people free must be based on principles in order to be effective in the freeing process.

It is also essential that the principles be based on what is right and wrong, what is good and bad, and what is true and false. In order to evaluate the truth of something, a person must be taught what truth feels like. They must be told what truth is and have been exposed to it. They must also have been exposed to false principles and be able to discern the difference between the two.

If the responsibility of a parent were broken down to its simplest description, it would be to teach children what is good and bad, right and wrong, and true and false in a safe, inspiring environment in order to make them masters of themselves. I think all parents want children to be confident stewards of their own lives. But, what many parents don't know is that being over-indulgent, or not teaching enough about the above mentioned core principles of learning, but letting the child "figure life out on their own" is not a gift, but rather a large obstacle to over-come.

Children of modern progressive parents are not free even though the parents are hoping freedom will be the result of the parenting choice. Parents wanting to give children opportunity with modern progressive methods will usually end up bewildered and frustrated at the actions the child chooses. This method of parenting is destructive by nature and frustrating for all involved.

### Bullying Fear-Based Parenting

Bullying fear-based parenting is an aggressive form of parenting which is also destructive for family relationships. It looks like: belittling, yelling, pushing, dragging, accusing, bossing, and striking. In this style the children have very little choice, if any. Parents are at war against disobedience. They will win the war at all costs.

Fear is an important part of this kind of parenting since it is the actual motivation for the children to comply. The parents feel that fear of parents is a healthy and proper motivation since the parents are bigger than the children. The parents probably chose to live productive lives out of fear and assume it is the most healthy motivation. Bully parenting isn't about what you are supposed to be or do, it is about what you are *not* supposed to be or do.

### Traditional Strict Parenting

Traditional strict parenting is different than the other styles because it is productive instead of destructive. It acknowledges choice within a structure, which is built around principles of virtues and morals that you, the parents, believe in. What principles are most important for your family to live by at this time? This will be referred to again later.

Ideas may include principles like: hard work creates confidence and happiness, polite behavior is a sign of respect for family relationships, effective communication needs to be learned not assumed – And there are many, many more. Think of the principles in which you believe. Make a list and then prioritize them. The principles or virtues which come to the top of the list are usually the ones your family needs to spend the most time learning.

Even if you don't know yet how to teach your family these principles the list will be your guide and help you determine when you have found the answer you are looking for. Assessing, prioritizing, planning and then taking action is self-government.

If you don't know what principles to put on your list yet, that's okay too. Your main focus needs to be exposing yourself to depth. Read classical inspired writings and discuss openly with people who you want to be like. As you surround yourself with greatness, you will see the great principles you need in order to change your heart. When your heart is changing, then your child can also experience a change of heart. It is impossible to teach something which you haven't experienced yourself.

Traditional strict parents know that relationships are based upon truth, vision and respect, so they regularly expose their families to truth, create a vision for their families to focus on, and teach skills within a structure which promotes respect.

progressive house is the point of real concern. The line which supports the roof, which represents the unified family structure, is an illusion. It is represented above with a dotted line. The unified family structure is an illusion because the parents think that trying to be their child's friend will create unity in the family, but it doesn't. Friendly behavior is good, but good parenting is bound by standards and principles. Friends let each other do whatever they want to, parents can't.

Likewise, the two dot lines on the top of the house representing teaching correct principles and correcting behaviors are an illusion. The parents are hoping that the friendship or leniency will promote obedience and allow for natural life lessons to be learned organically. I am convinced that if we could have learned all we needed to on our own, without parents, God would not have given us parents. We do have instincts, but wisdom is learned by principle.

### Bullying Fear-Based Mode and Movement

The mode of bullying fear-based parenting is that relationships are *animalistic;* "king of the hill" mentality. "I'm bigger than you, so I'm in charge!" This destructive form of parenting promotes survival of the fittest societies. It is power based and very aggressive. It causes helplessness and depression, a feeling of being lost, uncared for, and devalued. The movement of the bullying and fear-based parenting form is *backwards*. Relationships regress. This is the only direction of movement possible because of the damage the attitudes and behaviors cause the relationships.

Since the relationships are power based each person is often literally pulling the other family members *back*. It seems to be common sense that you can't get ahead unless someone else is pulled back.

In this image of the bullying house you will notice that the foundation and side walls are optimistically the same as described above for the modern progressive house. However, the roof is different. Notice that teaching and correcting are happening, but without a unified family structure

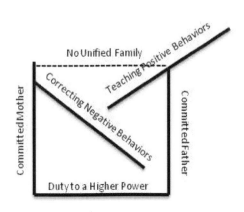

based on correct principles, the correcting makes the house fall in on itself. The family is completely unprotected and vulnerable to destruction.

Making a unified family government with working family meetings and input, which is mentioned in my book, *Parenting A House United*, is essential for teaching children correct principles. Without such a structure the family is in danger of power struggling with each other until someone wears down.

### Traditional Strict Mode and Movement

Throughout the years and cultural shifts associated with those years, the word strict has changed. Most people associate the term with the aggressive bullying form of parenting. Strict used to mean governing yourself or others by a set of virtuous principles. It has been proven that the best parents still do this. So, traditional strict parenting means being a *principle based* parent.

The movement of bullying parenting is backward and the movement of modern progressive parenting is forward. So, is traditional strict parenting stuck somewhere in the middle? No, traditional strict parenting moves *inside* each person in the family. It is about each person's ability to self-govern. The teaching revolves around bringing people to this end, and it trusts that with strict principles and a structure based on love, acceptance, trust, mercy and effective communication skills a self-governing family can be realized.

Strict parenting moves *inside*. It is all about changing children's hearts. It is not merely behavior modification, or how to get them to do what you want them to do. It is teaching children to see what the causes are and what the effects will be and then to make a choice if they want to change the consequences. Since children, like adults, have agency, they need to be taught how to use that agency – that choosing - wisely from the inside out. Traditional strict parenting is historical and based on moral order.

I have seen people embrace modern progressive parenting ideologies in an effort to be more "organic" in their parenting approach. The parents don't like getting mad and want calmness, and see friendly social behavior as the key to this goal. This desire for the most natural, the most foundational kind of parenting is good. However, modern progressive parenting is not the answer. It left moral order and virtuous principles long ago.

Traditional strict parenting is the only "organic" parenting style there is.

When I plant a seed and want to have a tree that is beautiful and productive, I must nourish it, water it, brace it, train it in its growth, give it everything it needs to be strong, to weather the storms, and to bear fruit. *That* is "organic". *That* is what parents were meant to do with and for their children. Children are born to parents, not to society, to teachers, or to the government. Parents offer nourishment for their child's happiness and self-government in their lives and in their social successes and interactions.

A friend recently confided in me about the problems she has noticed with her teenage daughter. The daughter often whines and pouts to try to manipulate those around her. The mother was justifiably concerned. She said, "Nicholeen, I know I have to do something, I have tried to be understanding to her problems and build her up, but it isn't working. In fact, as I look at the situation, I think I might be making it worse."

What a wise mother! She is right. This mother loves her daughter and wants her to be happy. When her child expressed desires the mother did what she could to satisfy the teenaged child. The child was essentially spoiled even though mother wouldn't normally be seen as the kind of parent who coddles, or babies her daughter. The spoiling happened by allowing the child to emotionally control everyone around her. This spoiling led to an unhappy habit.

After realizing the problem, the mother said to me, "I need to be more deliberate huh? I see that now. I need to never let her see that the manipulating behavior works!" In that one moment my friend began a journey toward being a traditional strict mother instead of a modern progressive one.

This image of a properly built house symbolizes the traditional strict parenting family. They are grounded on correct principles and have a commitment to a higher power, they have committed parents, a united family structure, and consistent teaching and correcting to promote good decision making and happiness.

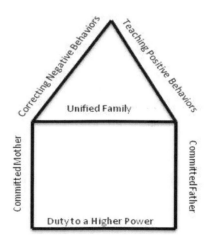

# 5

# LEADERSHIP STRUCTURE

### Modern Progressive Leadership Structure

Each of the three forms of parenting has their own unique leadership structure. The modern progressive leadership structure is *child-led*. The parents generally act as managers of chaos, which there tends to be a lot of because of the disconnection between the child and the parents. Management is not able to have proper parenting impact; it is servitude, child-led, and tyrannical (the child being the tyrant).

Often I have heard parents tell me that their three-year-old is in charge of the house! Three-year-olds should not be in charge of the house! Neither should thirteen-year-olds for that matter. Parents are in charge of keeping the family focused on true principles and learning effective skills. So, essentially the principles are in charge of the self-government home.

I have noticed that modern progressive parents are very good at facilitating. They facilitate entertainment and opportunities to keep their children busy and pacified. Facilitating is usually seen as the main responsibility of parenting. The parents all gather together on the sides of the soccer field, or the back of the music studio and discuss the strains of facilitating.

While soccer lessons and music lessons etc. are not wrong, they can be over done or be allowed to re-organize family priorities if not monitored carefully. Parents were not meant to merely be facilitators for their children. Parents were meant to mold, discuss, plan and prepare the children to happily succeed in life. These responsibilities take adequate connection time.

### Bullying Fear-Based Leadership Structure

Just as modern progressive parenting is tyrannical, so is bullying fear-based parenting. This probably doesn't come as much surprise since most people spend their whole parenting lives trying *not* to be this kind of parent for this very reason. If you remember, the tyrant in the modern progressive form of parenting is the child, but the tyrant in bullying fear-based parenting is the parent.

There is *no leader* in the bullying fear-based parenting form, just an out-of-control bully, a dictator, enforcer, but certainly not a leader. The attitude in this parenting style is generally: "Parenting is a battle, and I will win!" The home becomes a war zone.

It is probably easy to see why parenting should not to be that way. Parenting is a relationship which is wrapped in principles which create love and enduring affections.

### Traditional Strict Leadership Structure

The leadership structure for traditional strict parents is modeling by *parents*. The leader is the parent, and the parent models leadership.

In our religious household, we all read our scriptures individually in the evening before bed. Every morning we meet and discuss what we all read the night before and the principles we found. This small morning structure moment motivates the children to do their reading before they turn out the light so they can be prepared to comment each day. Even before the children could read, they wanted me to read scriptures to them at night so they could say something like Mom and Dad and the big kids do. This type of modeling has encouraged my family to enjoy scripture study and family scripture discussion as well. We have made similar modeling opportunities for behaviors and learning important life skills.

Another way parents model leadership is how they handle discipline. When parents are calm and act deliberately while correcting a child when something has gone wrong, then the children are more likely to be calm and act deliberately when something goes wrong in their lives as well. Parents have the privilege and the responsibility to teach their children certain skill sets based on righteous principles, which all members of the family know. This is modeling leadership. The most basic skills I teach and model are called "The Four Basic Skills." They teach children how to follow instructions, accept no answers and criticism, accept consequences, and disagree appropriately.

Modeling is a mindset. It is a way you see your role as a parent. If you see yourself as the example of what to do, then you are more likely to assert yourself and take deliberate action to train your children correctly. Leading the family in this way solves many house-hold and relationship problems. For instance, if you take time to work with your children daily instead of just assign work and have expectations then your children will learn how to do the job effectively and up to standard in a stress free, nurturing environment, while also building confidence and creating a vital connection with their parents.

This is not to say that children can't do chores independently. They need to learn that vital skill too, but they more quickly get to that skill level when they have been coached, taught and nurtured by their parents through the learning process.

My friend, Sherri Bowthorpe says, "Behaviors, both good and bad are contagious. Children learn things just by being there. Take driving for instance. Most children learn the basics of driving while being in the car with Mom or Dad and observing what is happening. The driving manuals only add details to the knowledge they already have." I have noticed this contagiousness to be true as well. Children who use bad language or don't budget their time effectively, often times have parents who do the same.

# 6

# TEACHING

## Modern Progressive Teaching

One day, while talking to an acquaintance about parenting I said, "I look at my role as parent as a sort of teacher. To me parenting is much more than just a disciplinarian." This woman looked at me strangely and was obviously not used to the idea of thinking of herself this way.

I was deep into fostering teenagers who had many skills to learn, and applied the parenting principles I learned doing foster care to teaching my young toddlers as well. I spent a good portion of every day evaluating what I was doing as a parent and if I was teaching correct principles. This mother had a couple young babies and hadn't really seen herself as more than a facilitator yet.

People need teaching. Without teaching we would all be similar to the "yahoos" in Gulliver's Travels, listening only to our bodies and our appetites. Teaching children is common sense. Why then do we not take that part of our parenting more seriously?

Just as my friend Sherri said above, "behaviors are contagious." This means that wheather we want to or not, as parents, we *are* teaching our children; either for the good, or the bad.

Those who practice modern progressive parenting may have a house with a foundation, but the roof of security and relationships are probably invisible. Teaching and correcting children gives the whole family safety and connective relationship building moments.

If the family is completely child-led and there is a *meager amount of teaching or correcting* of any kind, then where and how do relationships develop? The children have essentially been abandoned. They are on their own to figure out what is right and what is wrong. The world is viewed as subjective. Right and wrong vary depending on what you want and how you feel.

Not only are right and wrong confusing and misrepresented in modern progressive parenting, the authority on what is right and what is wrong is also surprising. Modern progressive parents look to society and the law as their authority for definitions of what is right and what is wrong. If it is illegal it is wrong. If it is legal it is right. If society considers it productive or responsible, it is good. If society considers it wasteful, selfish, or distracting then it is bad. Morals, or who defines morals, aren't really brought into the conversation.

For instance, years ago people thought it was good to put preservatives into food to prolong shelf-life and possibly increase the nutrition of the people because they can get good food when it is not in season or freshly made. In recent years, there has been a cultural movement to get the preservatives out of many foods. The same preservatives that used to be considered good are now being called bad because many health conditions have been linked to their consumption.

I know this issue doesn't have much to do with parenting - or does it - but, hopefully we see that if we let society determine what is good and what is bad, we will always end up confused. This food debate goes on inside people's minds every time they go to the store or are offered food. The only way to resolve the debate for yourself is to base your decisions on true principles. But, what if your parents never told you what was true and what was false? Well, then there is more confusion.

When I was young, I craved independence. I didn't want anyone telling me what to do. I was also pretty strong-willed, and saw people who bowed to other people's wishes as weak. I embraced all the independence I could and fought for more. I never needed or wanted anyone else's help. Society had shown me that the goal was to do it all yourself, and that true independence meant happiness. That was what I wanted.

I learned my independence lessons well and so was quite proficient. I was independent and confident; and my parent's most difficult child. Surprisingly, just when it seemed I had learned my lesson about independence fully, they were trying to take it away by telling me I couldn't do whatever I wanted to. I was confused and frustrated. For many years, I didn't talk to Mom and Dad much about my life, except for the minor scheduling things. My school teachers and people in society seemed to want me to be independent for most my life, and then suddenly my independence bothered my bully type parents. My social training and my parenting were in direct opposition. No wonder we didn't get along when I was a teenager at first.

The goal for modern progressive teaching is independence.

### Bullying Fear-Based Teaching

Why did my parents combat my social teachings about independence with power struggling? Simple. As described above, the opposite of modern progressive is bullying fear-based parenting. And, the language of fear-based parenting is power struggling. That is how the teaching is done. It was completely natural for my parents to go against the principle of indulgence and selfishness; these are incorrect principles. The natural choice was control, and it was taught by force.

It is important to note that my heart did not ever change because of this force. However, there were times when I later realized I should have been ashamed of my actions, but these feelings always came from thinking and sorting out feelings and a commitment to love my parents despite our disagreement. At home they taught us many truths. Our home was built upon gospel principles and was a loving place unless one of us was disrespectful or too opinionated. Disrespect was not tolerated. And, it shouldn't be. They were right about that.

The only time they resorted to fear-based parenting was when they didn't know what else to do about our disrespectful behaviors. They didn't know how to teach us a skill to disagree appropriately like I teach my children. At the time I was raised, it was most common to either be modern progressive or bullying fear-based parents. Traditional strict parenting was not taught at the time. I think my parents were traditional strict by nature and practice most of the time, but resorted to bullying when disrespectful or lazy behaviors surfaced.

In bullying fear-based parenting there is *no connection and no open communication* – a poorly constructed roof on the family house-- and it crumbles a little more with each storm of contention. So every time you try to teach and correct your children, the wind coming in from the storm pushes you down. There is no shelter and no security for anyone in the family.

Unlike modern progressive parenting there *is* a definite right and wrong. What is right and what is wrong is determined by the dictator/parent. If the parent is bothered or frustrated the action is wrong. The parents don't take any time to seek to understand the child. Instead they solve the behavior problem by verbally or physically attacking the person to quiet them.

Bullying fear-based parents practice positive legalism, which means that something is legal if the parent likes the action and approves, and illegal if the action is not pleasing to the parent. Bully parents are often very picky and have a habit of making big deals out of small issues. They are really consistent about finding behaviors which need to be fixed. In fact, these kinds of parents have a tendency to fault find to an extreme. There is a difference between fault finding and teaching. Teaching is much more. It involves praising, preparing, correcting, and calming a learning child.

The goal of bullying fear-based parenting is co-dependence. The ruler wants to maintain control for as long as possible because it makes her happy and secure. The future of the child is always related to the contentment of the ruler.

### Traditional Strict Teaching

Remember that simple traditional strict parenting house above? The foundation is labeled, "duty to a higher power". When the family is based on true principles and there is a committed mother and father who holds the entire house up the home has a firm foundation. The floor and walls of the home are the family relationships and the connecting point which holds the roof of the house firmly in place. And the top, or rafters and roof, are the *teaching and correcting* aspects of a solid family structure.

Teaching and correcting children are the parts of parenting that most people focus on. These are the practical day-to-day moments when parents hope to mold and instruct their child for future relationship success.

Traditional strict parents lead the family based on core values and principles. They teach the children what is right and wrong, true and false, and good and bad, which are learned from the parent's core beliefs. Religion is a vitally important aspect to core value teaching. God determines what is right and wrong, good and bad, true and false for traditional strict parents. There is no leniency in God's law. However, there is also no tyrant. God's principles are taught by consequences. Traditional strict parents teach the same.

Traditional strict parents know that families are forever. The family relationships are extremely important. The environment at home is not about being friendly or being right, it is about being united.

Being united requires understanding that we can't be happy and successful all by ourselves. We need supportive people around us. We need love and relationships. No one is ever happy without successful family relationships. They are our basic security and our strength in hard times.

If parents and children all need each other for happiness and recognize their family as the means to happy living then they are more committed to learning self-government and communicating effectively. Acknowledging that we need each other for success and happiness and living in a way where we honor and respect each other and our relationships, is called interdependence. The teaching goal for traditional strict families is interdependence.

# 7

# FOUNDATIONAL PRINCIPLE

### Modern Progressive Foundational Principle

In modern progressive parenting the foundational principle is *entitlement.* The children are entitled to make their own choices, entitled to have all the things they need to keep up with society, and entitled to have non-oppressive friends instead of parents. The result is that the children feel isolated, lonely, and burdened, as well as confused because there are too many choices. They are in a one-man rubber raft, bouncing from wave to wave and getting nowhere fast.

Modern progressive children are free from correction and encouraged to pave their own trail in life. They are flooded with stories and comments about the importance of identity and making your own identity. They want to be different from normal, while still being the same as all their peers. They are looking for their identity and the parents are facilitating all they can to help the child decide who they are.

The irony is that modern progressive parenting is identity based, but the children often end up with no identity. Because, as we know, identity is based upon purpose. Without core values and proper moral teaching children will not see anything wrong or right and will consequently not feel a sense of mission, or purpose in life.

### Foundational Principle: Bullying Fear-Based

The foundational principle in bullying fear-based parenting is *punishment.* It is retaliation or having a feeling of resentment towards a child. The result of this punishment principle is fear, dishonesty, and distrust.

Not long ago, I witnessed a parent angrily say to her son, "Why are you wearing those clothes? I told you, you couldn't wear those clothes..." The child was suddenly defensive and blatantly dishonest to his mother in order to protect himself. The mother continued the rage. Then I saw the boy emotionally retreat by pouting and shut down. How could this boy trust his mother? Without trust, a parent cannot teach anything of value.

It is very easy to slip into either the bullying fear-based or the modern progressive parenting modes. In our home we have had foster children who have done horrid things that I didn't even know existed before they came. I found myself thinking, "You repulse me." Could I parent this child with that condition of heart? No.

When it was time for one of my foster children to come home from school, I would look at the clock and think, "Five more minutes, and she will be home." I hated that feeling of dread; it would eat at me. I could make no positive impact on her with that resentful attitude. I was not parenting her at all! I cared about my comfort too much; her situation felt too hard for me some days. In both of these cases, I slipped into a modern progressive or bullying fear-based mode. I allowed the child to bother me so much that I just didn't care anymore. I had to change my attitude.

I don't know if you get the same feeling in your stomach that I do when I am upset. Mine feels like a big knot. And, I know that if I just yell, or kick something I will feel a release. However, I also know I will feel out-of-control and regret words said and actions I've taken. I am not willing to damage my relationships for selfish actions which only manipulate my body chemicals.

I am more than a body. I will not yell at other people and get angry, because it damages me spiritually and physically as well as damages my relationships with others, which are more important than any chemical release moment I might feel I need. I decided a long time ago that situations are not about me and what I feel, but my self-government is. So, I can choose happiness, understanding, love and self-control.

When you are tempted to give up or give in, scream and slam doors, or aggressively demand obedience, stop! Get a grip and fight that feeling. Analyze your emotions, do whatever you need to do to get in control and into calmness, and then make a change.

Bullying parenting is anger-based. The anger promotes the damaging words and actions. Calmness is the key to changing the base and improving the focus.


### Foundational Principle: Traditional Strict

With traditional strict parenting the foundational principle is *consequences*. This means using cause and effect and showing them what happens when children make good choices, and what happens when the choices are not good. In this way you give the children structure; they feel safe, they feel loved, and they feel a connection to you.

When the BBC show was filmed James and Hannah both changed their behaviors dramatically in one day. One day they were angry and trying to power struggle, and the next day they were calm and teachable. Why? Because they learned cause and effect. They tried power struggles and it didn't work. They had to try something else. The only response that worked and allowed them to be heard and understood in our home was calmness, so they chose that. I still remember Hannah saying, "Well, at my house if I yell I get my way, or someone at least yells back. But, here you are just so calm. It didn't work, so I chose to be calm too."

By nature people look for what works to get what they want. We all try to manipulate the law of cause and effect each day by adding emotional elements to the situation. If it works we keep manipulating, but if it doesn't, we ultimately find what does work. In a traditional strict home, true principles are what works.

As a side note, many parents wonder why their child is obedient for school teachers and other adults and not for them. Cause and effect is the answer again. A parent's responses train the child to create a habit of connecting a certain way, even if it is destructive to the relationship. So, don't give in, give up, or power struggle. All these behaviors encourage bad relationship habit forming.

# 8

# FOCUS

## Modern Progressive Focus

The focus of modern progressive parenting is *self-discovery*, and it is a failure. It is human nature to want to know who we are and what we were meant for. People have been trying to figure that question out for years. Some people spend their whole lives trying to figure this question out, while others are taught the answers to these questions in their youth and quickly understand that their lives are about much more than themselves.

Think of the person you admire most. Who do you want to be like? I've noticed that I'm trying to be like people who love and serve God and live to do His will. I'm trying to be like people who care about humanity and finding truth. I'm trying to be like people who recognize relationships as sacred and respect and love all humanity. I'm trying to be like people who stand for something even when it isn't popular, and who actively invite others to join them. My list could go on and on. But, the important thing is that none of the people I'm trying to be like are caught up in themselves. They are ready to do things because they are past the self-discovery phase.

Not knowing who you are and what you were meant for is dangerous. Such a person can be influenced heavily by the media and popular thought. They are not really free to think like they want to. Their perspective on life is limited and they often feel small and unimportant. This is why modern progressive children often make many mistakes in life. They are drifting and don't have a harbor to offer safety and focus.

Drifting involves making bad choices just to see if they really are bad. It involves doing something wrong because it might give you a clue to who you are. It *might* cause some sort of feeling that will make a change or give direction. Even if it has been said to be dangerous, it is irrelevant if it can give a person an event to attach identity to.

## Bullying Fear-Based Focus

The focus of bullying fear-based parenting is *self-preservation*. Being self-preservation minded is physically, spiritually, and especially emotionally destructive and, therefore, is a failure as well.

I met a girl one time that lived a secret life. No one really knew her. She didn't share much information because she wasn't sure who to trust. She seemed shy and uninterested in friendship. She had a hard time being in groups and kept most of her conversations to pleasantries. She carried secrets and fears. Secrets about her past and how she was treated by her parent and fears that someone would abuse her trust and love again. My friend was consumed with preserving herself emotionally and physically and didn't know another way to live.

It all started with an abusive parent who made threats, told lies, manipulated, and got physical. My friend, she felt alone and vulnerable. She wasn't sure who she could trust. Her life has been terribly scarred by an aggressive parent. Even to this day she has a hard time making friends, doesn't open up to people, and feels vulnerable.

As a side note she says she has a problem with losing control while parenting her children. She has made great efforts to stop yelling and swearing and doing things she shouldn't, but has a hard time not falling back into the way parenting was modeled for her.

I admire this woman greatly. She is a pioneer. She is changing her ways. She is learning self-government and is raising different kinds of children than she was. I pray for her success. It is hard to break a habit, but it is possible.

## Traditional Strict Focus

The focus of traditional strict parenting is *family unity*. It is not focused on the self of the parent or the self of the child. It's about this collective group – Father, Mother, and children - making a home together, and the family's purpose as a group; its mission.

Have you ever noticed that when people get old their favorite subject to talk about is their family? I have. They tell story after story, family accomplishment after family accomplishment because they know their families are the most important part of life and have the greatest value in today's world.

We can learn from the focus of our elders on their families. If, at the end of their lives, family relationships are more valuable than anything else, then we need to value them all along. We shouldn't wait until we are nearing the end of our lives to strive for strong family relationships. Family unity should be a daily focus now.

# 9

# AGENCY

## Modern Progressive Agency

I believe the greatest power we have has human beings is our agency. We have a power to choose. It is this very God-given power that makes us free. Author Victor Frankl showed the world this truth in his book *Man's Search For Meaning* that no one can take away your freedom as long as you have the power to choose. This power is born in all of us and needs to be taken into consideration by parents. A wise parent knows that creating a structure where good choices are obvious and preferable is the only way to really help someone want to choose right. Any other method is abandonment or manipulation, and goes directly against agency.

Some may wonder how abandonment goes against agency. Well, in order to make right choices the person has to know what right choices actually are. Leaving someone all alone to choose, like modern progressive parenting does, compromises a person's agency as well. We always have agency, but it can only protect us and strengthen us when we know what is right and what is wrong, and as described earlier, right and wrong must be taught.

Modern progressive parents give their children complete license and by so doing give them confusion. Choices become unpredictable. Success must be gained by trial and error; and often isn't found altogether, especially in relationships.

I can't remember who said it, but it is true, "Why learn from your own mistakes, when you can learn from the mistakes of others?" People who are aware of what is right and what is wrong don't usually make the same mistakes they have seen many other people make.

## Bullying Fear-Based Agency

Similarly, bullying fear-based parents also encourage their children to learn by trial and error because they change the law so often to fit their whims and behave so oppressively. When a person feels oppressed they try to find ways to feel freedom so they 'play systems.'

'Playing systems' is nothing more than trying to find a weak spot to steal freedom. It is a different version of trial and error. Children who have been bullied are afraid to doing something wrong, but are looking for a way to have power too. They have been shown that the only way to win the relationship battle is to get power any way you can. The children can't wait to be big enough to not be bullied any more. Then they can bully who they want to and have power.

Bullying fear-based parenting takes opportunities to use agency away from the children. They still have some, but since it isn't based on what is right and wrong their choices end up looking more like manipulations. In the chart comparing the three styles of parenting (page 16 and 17), we have chosen to say that in this form of parenting children have no agency; meaning they base their choices on which manipulation will work best in a given situation.

### Traditional Strict Agency

Traditional strict parenting is liberty based. Since the parenting is founded on true principles and skills which lead to effective, loving communication, the family has the support it needs to be truly free. Liberty means knowing. Knowing is freedom. The root of the word liberty is *liber*, which actually means "book," or to read write and speak. You may notice how library and liberty have the same Latin root. What do we get out of books? Knowledge. What do traditional strict parents focus on giving their children? Knowledge. Their parenting is free and liberty-based parenting.

Since traditional strict parenting is based on liberty it is very predictable. Children and parents are both using skills based on principles which make learning cause and effect easy. The family knows what will happen if they choose one way or another and have no anxiety over the family structure. When a person has been grounded in what is right and wrong then there is no confusion about where happiness comes from, and obedience is chosen as a means to that happiness and family connection.

# 10

# PARENTING ACTION

## Modern Progressive Parenting Action

Action is a manifestation of the heart of the person. I know we all make action mistakes from time to time and work to correct them, but I also know that the only way to make sure the action doesn't happen again is to strengthen the heart.

So what can we learn about the heart of each of the three kinds of parents?

Modern progressive parents act in an ignoring way to their children. They ignore the teaching which can strengthen the child, and ignore the effects from many actions. Ignoring is a wild behavior. As stated above, some may like to call it organic, but looking closely, it is easy to see it is wild. The product, or child, is uncultivated, unrestrained, and unproductive. When a person is used to being unrestrained by principle they are like water; ever flowing to the lowest point.

I had a mother come up to me one day and say, "Your son and my son are the same ages, but they are so different. Your son is on political campaigns and writing books and running businesses. I just hope my son will get off of his computer games for an hour per day. Do you think there is hope for my son?"

I felt the concern this mother had. She had given her child all she could. She facilitated so many activities and experiences. She got him the electronics he wanted and lovingly hoped for the best for him. Then he, day after day, just went the easiest route; the path of least resistance.

In my family we call this the P.L.R. We know the P.L.R. is destructive and avoid it like the plague. We talk about it and correct the children if they find themselves following that path. On purpose, I ask my children, "what are you doing that is useful?" They are used to thinking like this and now are not happy if they are lazing about.

Why do children learn to take the P.L.R.? Usually it is because their parents use the P.L.R. Even if the parent is a work-horse, if they are doing 'it all' themselves, the child is not being taught productivity so the child becomes comfortable with not taking responsibilities. According to them, responsibilities are for other people.

### Bullying Fear-Based Parenting Action

By contrast, bullying fear-based parenting is very demanding. All action is required. The parent is unyielding; much like a rock. The parent is an obstacle not a nurturer. They are something to work around and watch out for, not someone to respect.

Rocks smash things, they don't nurture and produce. A rock-type parent demands productivity without planting seeds. They are consumptive. Their focus is on how they are affected. And, since this is the focus, rock parents inspire their children to also be selfish and in no time they are rock children with illusions of strength, passively waiting for their next battle.

### Traditional Strict Parenting Action

Seeds cannot grow in water, and will not grow on rocks. They grow in soil; the richer the better. Traditional strict parents see themselves as rich soil. They nourish their little seeds and train them up as they grow. Their parenting action is to be inspiring.

The child chooses correct principles because the tone and structure of the home inspire that kind of self-government.

Since the parent is aware of his nurturing role, he constantly cultivates himself and nourishes himself, just as a good gardener amends the Fall soil for a strong Spring crop. The parent sees himself as the reason the child will choose self-government. He is the leader; the example of happy living. Even if his life is not ideal, he constantly focuses on what he can control; himself and what his role as parent means. A person who understands their role is focused and ready to inspire others.

# PART 3

# YOUR
# CULTURAL PARENTING
# REVOLUTION

# 11

# CPR:
# CULTURAL PARENTING REVOLUTION

The world we live in preaches a doctrine of selfishness. There are so many distractions which are pulling family members away from their families to lives more self-absorbed. What would happen to our societies if this changed? What if families healed and focused on uniting again? We would have a family revolution.

In order to have a family revolution, there needs to be a parenting revolution. Revolutions are moments when citizens stand up and say, "no" to social norms and peer pressure. They are moments in history when the citizens are assertive and will not be bullied by fears and worries. They are moments when citizens look inside themselves and see a God-given power to choose what is right.

It is time for just such a revolution. Our families are under attack. Darkness and confusion are encircling our families and our communities. Tragedy abounds. People are asking themselves what they can do about it all. Focus on what counts; the family and your relationships.

When there are problems in the world it is always wisest to look for the nearest place you can have an impact for good. Those nearest places are you and your family.

### What We Can Do
If you need help preparing for your parenting revolution you can find many helpful books and audio classes, as well as our own ten-step Implementation Course to help you make your transition smoothly.

### Traditional Strict – The Best Style!
On our chart, the first two parenting methods, modern progressive and bullying fear-based are destructive. The bottom one, traditional strict, is constructive; it builds good people using cause and effect. Discuss your

parenting goals and your new direction openly with your family; have family meetings regularly and start implementing the list. If things are not going well, you can get help. Be deliberate and vigilant in your parenting. When things get tough, resist the temptation to slip back into old ways that destroy relationships. Pray for courage, direction and help.

My family has been very deliberate and very vigilant in our parenting, and I can promise you that when your children gather around and hold onto the truth and correct principles that pour from every movement and every conversation you have, it is sweet, and they are happy. They achieve things you never thought possible.

# 12

## ESPECIALLY FOR HUSBANDS

Women contact me and my husband all the time asking how to help fathers become unified with mothers. Apparently, it is rather common for husbands and wives to have different ideas about parenting.

This is a message for the men; the husbands. My husband's style of parenting used to be aggressive, the bullying fear-based kind. He was in bully mode 100% of the time, and was 100% successful in repelling our children. They always went to me first before they went to him. But, he was sad, because he did not want his children to be afraid of him. His desire and his method did not match, but he thought that being soft was unmanly and would not be effective. Here is one of his "turn around" experiences that he had with our son:

### From Bossing to Loving

"I used to read scriptures or a story with my son at night before he went to bed. When he guessed at a word, I always declared, "That's not right. Do that word again!" Pretty soon he didn't want to read with me anymore. I was troubled about that and eventually realized that I had to change the way I read with him. I came up with a plan, something I would do when he didn't say a word correctly. I decided that I would give him a hug or tickle him (He loves to be tickled). So when we were practicing his little flashcards, I did just that. Pretty soon that cycle started to turn around because he felt more comfortable with me, and I enjoyed reading with him more."

He continues: "The constant correcting I was doing was bullying. It caused discouragement and emotional distance in my son. I noticed and made a plan to change the outcome. If I could give a piece of advice it would be to take time to look at your methods and the reactions of your children. They will tell you much! Turn things around by loving and cherishing your children. They will grow up to be you! Is what you are observing what you want?"

### The World's Strictest Parents: You Too?

When the BBC first asked me if I thought I was a strict parent, I didn't think I was. But, now I am pretty sure the title applies to my parenting perfectly, and I consider the title a compliment!

Strict parenting is the effective parenting of the past, and has also been proven to be the effective parenting of the future. True principles don't change. So many answers to life's problems are found through strictly following principles. I call this self-government.

# REFLECTION

I believe in assignments. The problem is people reading books don't often believe in doing them. So, I am going to create an awkward space right here for you to do the following assignment.

Answer the following questions:

1) What type of parenting do you currently find yourself doing?

2) What behaviors do you need to stop doing?

3) What do you need to do most to help heal your family right now?

4) Who, in your family, needs your attention most right now?

5) What should you parenting structure look like to support the type of parent you want to be?

6) What ten things does your family need to focus on first? (morals, virtues, principles, etc.)

**If you left the spaces above blank, fill them in now.**
**(No, really go back and do it.)**

Since you just took time to do some analysis, it is time to make a plan.

1) Does your structure and communication support your goals?

2) How will you present your ideas to the family?

3) What skills are you lacking?

If your structure or methods don't support your foundational list, then look for something that you can do to fix it. Look for new ideas. Look for mentors.

# ABOUT THE AUTHOR

 Nicholeen Peck is the mother of four and previous foster parent of many difficult and troubled teens. The Peck family's success with these difficult children was based upon calmness, the principles of self government, and good communication. She has been teaching people around the world the principles of Self-Government since 1999. In 2009, Nicholeen and her family were featured in a one hour BBC documentary about parenting. She has appeared on various news shows and radio programs to discuss effective parenting. She is a popular public speaker, author of the books, *'Parenting a House United'*, *'Londyn LaRae Says Okay'*, *'Porter Earns a Quarter'*, many magazine articles, and a blog called *'Teaching Self-Government'*.

Nicholeen owns the websites: TeachingSelfGovernment.com and ParentingSelfGovernment.com where she offers resources to master the Teaching Self-Government principles, system and skills in your home through newsletters, support groups, classes , audios and books.

# PARENTING RESOURCES

Go to **http://ParentingSelfGovernment.com** to sign up for Nicholeen's free parenting newsletter and explore the many articles posted on the site.

Other supporting products found on the site include:
> Audio classes, books, Seminar on CD, DVD's of Nicholeen coaching a large family in their cultural change, digital products, children's books that teach self-governance skills,
> and a Teaching Self Government community of Learning Circles, Forum participants, Retreats, and Instructors.

Most importantly, you'll find the
**10 Step Teaching Self Government Implementation Course**
that has been designed specifically to help families become peaceful and united through practical lessons, How-To Videos, Articles, Downloadable audio classes, and more, all designed to expand the principles in this book into practical steps and systems that help you change your family culture at your pace.

**Find the Implementation Course here:**
*(http://parentingselfgovernment.com/implementation-steps)*

**Follow Teaching Self Government on Facebook:**
**https://www.facebook.com/teachingselfgovernment**

Made in the USA
San Bernardino, CA
25 November 2014